STRATEGIC BUSINESS LESSONS FROM THE ANIMAL KINGDOM

How animal habits can make your business profitable, even if you know nothing about business strategy

Olumide Holloway

OTHER BOOKS BY THE AUTHOR

1. The Way of the Lion.
2. Smoking Guns and Bleeding Streets.
3. The Untold Story of Uriah the Hittite.
4. Storytelling the Book of Proverbs.
5. The Poetpreneur.
6. Love Letters from a Poetpreneur.
7. Darkness can be very dark.
8. How many NO, make a YES?

All the books are available on Amazon.

The books are also on www.wordup411ng.com, and do subscribe to the website to receive notifications of news and updates by email.

ABOUT THE AUTHOR

Olumide Holloway, better known as "Olulu, the King not from Zulu." is a 'POET-preneur', a writer, poet and a spoken word artist. He loves reading, writing, dancing, making people happy and generally having fun. He's passionate about Spoken Word Poetry, and his core purpose in life is to continually build capacity in people using the spoken word as a tool and medium.

He is the promoter of WORD UP (a foremost Spoken Word Poetry event in Nigeria), and War Of Words (Nigeria's biggest slam poetry competition).

He believes that people should do what they love, and love what they do. That way we can all be loving life, living in love, and getting paid for building businesses around our passion.

He is on Twitter @olulu4ever and on Instagram @olulutheking

DEDICATION

To the creator of nature and all we who are lifelong learners.

ACKNOWLEDGEMENT

Nat Geo WILD for their amazing content.

CONTENTS

ABSTRACT

Question: Olulu, why are you writing about animals?

Answer:
It is because one day my wife wanted to cook stew and she said I should help go to the market.
I asked, why me?
She asked, 'would you rather another man did it for me?'
So I went.
Another time, she asked me to drop her off somewhere off my route.
I said it wasn't convenient.
She asked if I would rather another man dropped her off.
So I drove her there and waited until she was ready to leave.
In the early hours of a new day, at about 4am. I rolled over to my wife and nudged her with my 'working stick'.
She said, no o, I need to get up early because of school runs and work.
'Should I call another woman?' I asked.

The above is the long answer to why I write about animals.

The short answer is simple: I'm a writer, so I write.

Drops mic...comes back to pick mic, and then drops the pen.

CHAPTER ONE

LION, CROCODILE AND HIPPOPOTAMUS

I'm a fan of the Nat Geo WILD.

The three animals I like to watch are Lion, Crocodile and Hippopotamus.

Why these three?

Because I finally understood SWOT analysis better from them.

Let's talk about the Lion.

What can man learn from this beast?

Well, God described himself as the Lion of Judah. Satan, the enemy is also called 'a roaring lion seeking for who to devour.'

Many sports teams and individuals also associate themselves with the Lion.

In the story of survival, the Lion never walks, I mean, never works alone, this we can term as a company/organisation/community (better known as a pride of lions).

Hunting for prey is a joint effort. Lionesses take the lead in the hunt, but when the prey is problematic, say a buffalo or giraffe and is difficult to bring down, then the Lion shows up. This signifies delegation of duties, collaboration and cooperation between members.

The Lion eats first, followed by the Lioness; then the cubs - this is a chain of authority.

Do you know lions also hunt and kill elephants? The Lion is bold, fearless and daring.

However, one animal the Lion is yet to (consistently and successfully) kill and eat is the Crocodile. A lion does not fear the Crocodile, but it never gets into the water after it.

Why?

The Lion recognise its own weaknesses. He is not a good swimmer and cannot stay underwater. So it acknowledges the Crocodile as a better beast in the water, and therefore a threat if the Lion ventures into deep water.

But, you know what is funny?

A crocodile will never ever dare a fully-grown hippopotamus in the water. Yet, lions despite their aversion for water hunt and kill hippos.

The Lion is known by its ability to strategise. It is no mean feat to kill a fully-grown elephant. Thus, the Lion usually bends (or breaks a little bit) its own rule to ensure the hunt is successful.

Knowing the rules to bend and the ones to break, and when to do so are referred to as actionable strategies in SWOT analysis.

CHAPTER TWO

PART TWO: LIONS, CROCODILES
AND HIPPOPOTAMUSES.

The only lesson a lion cub is taught is how to dominate. It fears no one and dares everyone. The tallest, biggest, and smallest animals are all prey in the eyes of a lion.

However, one beast which has dared the lion and lived to tell the tale and has yet to be (officially) killed by the Lion is the Crocodile, specifically, the Nile Crocodile.

Here is a fun fact about crocodiles: the biggest crocodile (in captivity) was measured (mouth to tail) at 20ft 3inches. Crocodiles are large animals, but size is not their biggest advantage.

The croc's two key strengths are the natural body armour on its back and the fact it has one of the most powerful bite forces in the world.

I once watched, on TV, four lions battling one crocodile and how their bites failed to penetrate its back. The Crocodile escaped into deep waters unharmed. In India, a tiger lost a tooth in a battle with a crocodile.

(Quickie: The Lion is not the biggest cat; the Tiger is bigger and more muscular than the Lion.)

If a crocodile bites you, there are only two ways of escape. One, by God's grace, which is that it turns into a vegetarian and releases you, and two, by God's grace, meaning you somehow get a detachable limb to put as a limb in its mouth.

The Crocodile mainly hunts in the water. So, one of its virtues is patience. It waits for the prey to come to it and then strikes with speed to grab a part of it.

One other thing about the Crocodile is its attitude, the knack for being aggressive and never backing down (well, except maybe when it faces a fully-grown hippopotamus). It fears no animal and dares almost all animals.

The opportunity it uses to maximise its strength is that all animals must drink water, so you come to it. It does not need to chase you.

So how do you make people come to you?

You know this saying that, you can force a horse to the river, but you can't force it to drink.

Well, your job is not to force the horse to do anything, your job is to make the horse thirsty, and it will naturally go to the water to drink.

So how do you make people thirsty for your services? Why do you think they serve you groundnut for free at bars and joints? The more groundnut you eat, the more beer you drink.

Like the Crocodile, provide incentives to make people seek you out. Find a way to make people come to you and once they do, apply your bite force to haul them in all the way. But make sure you have body armour (aka competitive advantage) to withstand the intrusion of competitors, aka lions.

Outside the water, the Crocodile is somewhat vulnerable. Except it is going for a dead animal, seeking another river or basking in the sun, it does not leave the water.

On land, it can't outrun any animal except maybe the tortoise, so it has learnt not to run, instead it's very patient. So sometimes, it stays hungry for days while waiting.

Can you wait? How long can you wait?

Learn to be patient, bid your time, don't lunge for your prey too soon.

CHAPTER THREE

I t's time to talk about the Hippo.

I find the Hippo interesting and worth studying because there are three or more unique things, which makes up its SWOT - strengths, weakness, opportunities and threats.

Of the three animals mentioned so far, the Hippo is the only non-flesh eating predator among them. Yet it has the weaponry of a flesh eater.

Hippos have large teeth: the lower canines and lower incisors are enlarged especially in males and never stop growing.

The incisors full length comes to 1ft 4 inches, while the canine comes to 1ft 8 inches. The canine is kept sharpened by constant vertical wear against the shorter upper canines. So the hippo's canines are sharper than a Samurai sword.

Hippos can open their mouth to a massive 4ft wide, which is capable of biting a 10ft crocodile in half as well as a small boat.

Hippos are aggressive and are considered very dangerous. Unfortunately, their young ones fall victim to the temper of adult Hippos. Does that ring a bell? Lack of anger management or inability to control emotions.

The inability to control your emotions can and will ruin your life if left unchecked. To limit or eliminate this weakness, you need to be emotionally intelligent. Emotional intelligence is the ability to make your emotions work for and not against you.

If you can't control your emotions, you lose control over everything around you. Like the Hippo, you will end up destroying those you love by doing too much or too little or acting rashly.

Emotions are not limited to anger. It can be a long list: greed, envy, jealousy or even low self-esteem, etc. So detect your weaknesses and deal with them, before your enemies (or competitors) find them and deal with you.

Hippos are social beasts, hanging out in groups consisting of ten or more. The group includes both sexes, and is usually led by a dominant male. The dominant male attains this status by winning in combat against other males. In most cases, it's the dominant male who has the (first, and sometimes sole) right to mate with females.

Being in a community is important, but learning to dominate your space is key. If you cannot dominate by mastering your area of expertise, you will always be submissive. And if you show ambition without the necessary skill and understanding, you could be forced out. No man is an island; life is living with others.

Let's go back to the Hippo's teeth. Remember that the lower canines are sharpened daily by wear against the upper teeth; so, its weapons are ever ready for battle. What are your weapons (i.e skills)? What do you do everyday to update your skills? What do you do everyday that keeps you in the mind of your (potential) customers, sponsors, investors etc.)?

The only hippo that gets (killed and) eaten easily by lions, hyenas and crocodiles are young hippos and dead hippos. No predator dares a herd of hippos and lives to tell the tale. Remember what I said about community, there is strength in numbers.

TEAM: Together Everybody Achieves More.

Hippos spend 16 hours in water and can stay submerged for 5 minutes or more. They don't swim; they paddle on the river bed with their legs. They are herbivores, so they go on land for food. If isolated on land, a pride of lions could get lucky and take down one hippo. But isolated or not, no predator hunts a matured hippo in water.

So, in closing, don't get isolated, stay in your area of expertise.

Dominate. Dominate. Dominate. Don't compete!!!

Sharpen your teeth. Sharpen your skills daily.
Don't be controlled by your emotions, control your emotions.

Earn the right to mate; I mean, to lead. (Don't get an erection if you are not the dominant male 😀😀😀).

Live life, before life leaves you.

CHAPTER FOUR

USING HYENAS TO UNDERSTAND SWOT.

Hyenas bear a close resemblance to dogs but are more related to the cat family than the canine. Either way, An hyena is neither a cat nor a dog.

It is smaller than a lion, slightly taller/ bigger than a leopard and has one of the strongest jaws in the animal kingdom. That simply means that if it bites your hand, that hand is no longer yours - blood, bone and skin. Hyenas eat even the horns and hoofs of its victims.

So how does an animal smaller than the Lion steal meat/food from it? First, let's talk about how it steals from the cheetah and the Leopard.

I once watched a leopard kill an antelope, and on sighting a hyena, it tried to climb the tree with its kill. But the tree was not near enough, and it can't outrun the Hyena carrying the dead meat. So it stood its ground ready to fight. Usually, if it was two hyenas, the Leopard would abandon the meat and run. But at that moment, it was one on one.

The Leopard is faster and has sharper claws than the Hyena. The jaws of the Hyena is supported by a thick skull. So the Hyena did not bother to start a catfight with the Leopard. It just head-butted the Leopard. The first time, the second time and the Leopard ran away.

Why head-butt?

If the Hyena had started the fight using its claws and mouth, the Leopard would have easily slashed its throat. But by head-butting, the Hyena protected its throat and in the same move, used one of its strongest parts, its skull, to daze the Leopard.

In another scene, four cheetahs were eating an animal they just caught, and a Hyena came calling. The cheetahs tried to chase the Hyena away. But it only took one step back, two steps forward. After a while, the Cheetahs left the meat for the hyena: no attack, no fight, just submission.

Why did the Cheetahs give up like that? Well, because cheetahs are built light, and their lives and hunting depend on their speed. Any injury to the Cheetah means it will die of hunger. The Cheetah can't afford an injury, and it is not heavy enough to withstand heavy brushing. So any predator bigger than the Cheetah will chase it away. The Hyena knows this and uses it time and time again.

Four things to decipher from the above are structure, skills, system and strategy. The Hyena has fighting skills; it has a strategy when faced with other predators. His strategy is based on the knowledge of self, knowledge of the market and knowledge of competitors. It has a structure; team/collaborators/ community/ company and each person understands and implements the system (system here means process flow).

So how do these four things work when the Hyena takes on the Lion?

When it comes to stealing meat from a Lion, and there is a face-off between one hyena and a lion, the endgame is that the hyena dies. If the scenario is that of two hyenas against one lion, the lion wins. Also if it is three hyenas vs a lion, the Lion wins. When it becomes four to one, the advantage switches.

I once read on Quora that, 'Cats are natural-born assassins.' The only reason your pet cat has not killed you is because you outweigh it 10 to 1 or more and you feed it, so it does not need to hunt. The most dangerous cat assassin is the lion. From "cubhood," until it becomes the dominant male, and until it dies, it is a killing machine.

When you face a bigger and stronger killing machine (competitor), The first thing you need is a structure, i.e. a team. Next, you need a workable strategy. After that, you need to outline and combine your skills. Lastly, understand, adopt and implement the above three into a system.

Let's go back to the four hyenas vs one lion. Particularly, a lioness. At four to one, hyenas will overpower lionesses, i.e. twenty hyenas to five lionesses.

The odd changes if there is one lion there. To overpower and out-wit one lion will depend on one key element. Is it an adult lion? If it is an adult lion, then more hyenas are required. It takes like fif-teen or more hyenas to route one lion. Remember, the older a lion is, the stronger and more experienced it becomes as an assassin. So the more experienced the lion, the more hyenas are needed.

As a lion, leverage on your knowledge, skill and experience; make them count. As a hyena, leverage on your structure/ team, aka collaboration and strategy, make them count.

The Hyena knows its weaknesses; it is not faster, bigger or more powerful than a ilon. So it has learnt not to leverage on power or speed but on strategy. Of course, it usually has some members of the pack who pay the ultimate sacrifice in implementing this system.

What is the strategy it uses for the Lion?

Get three or more members of the pack to distract the Lion, while the others snap and nip at the Lion's buttocks and hind legs. Any direction the Lion turns, have a few in front, and more behind. Usually, a lion will sit down to protect its balls just as you should always protect your valuables and assets as an individual or an organisation.

However, the Hyena knows its limitations. If there are two adult lions. The hyenas do not make an attempt. If they do, death is certain. There are markets with two dominant players; they will combine to force you out if you try to act like James Bond.

So in one sentence, I can summarise the above by saying:

'Don't use yesterday's anointing for today's miracles.'

In business terms...

Don't use the same strategy for every competitor/market/cus-tomer.

Study the market, make your plan, and execute it. However, know your limitations.

I hope with these few points; I've not confused you too much. If I did, well,...

CHAPTER FIVE

WHY CATS SHOULD NOT GET
NAKED WITH BABOONS

L et's go back to the cat family.

I can't get enough of them. So which of the cat family should we talk about?

This cat is the smallest of the four big cats. The other three are Tiger, Lion, and Jaguar.

This cat is the least social and the most elusive of the big African cats (jaguars are usually found in South America while India is the home for tigers).

This cat either ambushes its prey or stalks it as a hunting technique. It tries to get as close as it can to the prey. After which, it runs, pounces and kills the prey with a bite to the neck, all in one move. Sleek, right?

The key tactic of this cat is the element of surprise. Once the hunt turns to a foot race, the cat backs down.

This cat is called the Leopard.

It must compete for food and shelter with other large predators, e.g. Lions and Hyenas, who steal food from it and sometimes kill it.

Thus, Leopards co-exists with these bigger competitors by hunting for different types of prey and avoiding areas frequented by them. It will retreat up a tree in the face of direct aggression to hide and eat its food.

The Leopard's main prey is the Antelope. However, it has an ancient enmity with the Baboon. More on baboons later.

In any and every economy/market, there will be competition, and if you are upcoming and/or smaller than your competitors, you are in for a rough ride. But like leopards, you need to know and work on two things: market niche and market fit.

The Leopard will never hunt a buffalo, much less an elephant. It knows and respects its limitations. And because it lives with bigger competitors, it focuses on what they won't focus on.

Quickie: face your focus. Don't be distracted by what others are hunting. Don't take on more than your skill set can handle.

The Leopard carved out a market niche for itself; antelopes or smaller animals. Although lions hunt antelopes too; the larger the pride, the bigger the prey they need. Your large competitors won't want to waste resources serving 10 or 100 people when they can serve 1,000.

Dear reader, go for the 10, serve the under-served. Own the customers often ignored by others.

Market fit is providing the right product/ service for your market niche. That means that when you identify your niche, you must make sure you are able to provide the service it needs.

If a leopard gets lucky and kills a buffalo or bigger animal, it can never carry it up a tree. The food will go to its competitors. But with the right prey, it will easily go up the tree and eat in peace. Your product/service must satisfy or even exceed the expectations of your consumer.

Identifying your niche might be easy, getting the market fit is where the work is. The smaller the prey the Leopard chases, the faster the prey can run. And remember, the Leopard is not built for speed. So as a young leopard learning to hunt, you will miss plenty of prey. At some presentations, you will fumble and choke up. At some marketing calls, you will talk too much or too soon or not even make sense.

The young Leopard has a mentor, its mum. It watches and learns from her. As it grows, it mimics her action while playing. So whether a mentor adopts you or you adopt a mentor from afar, just get a mentor.

As earlier mentioned, leopards and baboons are mortal enemies. So don't be unevenly yoked with people who don't share your belief or philosophy. Study people and know them before you partner with them. or else, you might end up scarred or worse, dead.

One on one, the Leopard can kill a Baboon. But baboons usually gang up to attack a Leopard, and since leopards don't work in a group, the odds always favour the Baboons. An Arab proverb says; you can walk in front of your enemies (aka competitors) when hungry, but not when naked. Don't expose yourself to (ridicule by) anyone and everyone. Be guarded/ careful with who you get naked with. Be careful who you complain to or discuss your competitive advantage with.

Here are lessons to never forget from the leopard:
- Identify your market niche.

- Make sure you have the fit for the market.
- Focus on your focus.
- Serve the unserved.
- Be careful who you bare yourself to. Don't get naked in the wrong places.

CHAPTER SIX

HOW TO BECOME A PYTHON.

W hen a living, moving thing can average 17ft in length, and grow to be about 30ft, it is worth studying.

All muscles, no hands, no legs, no claws, no talons, and yet has continued to survive and thrive despite the different competitors for the same prey.

Let's talk about snakes. But not just any snake, our particular focus is on Mr P, the Python.

The Python (i.e. the Reticulated Python) is the longest snake in the world at 30 feet, closely followed by the Green Anaconda (species of the Boa Constrictor) at about 29 feet. But the Anaconda is almost twice as heavy.

We've been talking about focusing on your focus, so let's focus on the Python.

At an average size of 17 feet, it is a massive beast, now imagine a 30 feet beast.

Its diet includes lizards, rats, birds, other reptiles, and mammals. Mr P has been known to attack and kill humans. Yes, you read, correctly. You are on the menu list for this beast. (Did I hear you shout God Forbid?)

Pythons sit and wait for predators. They are difficult to detect and difficult to trap due to infrequent movements between hiding places. They can even live in urban areas easily.

They will generally attack any animal or human when they are hungry or are provoked. You often don't see them if you are not actively looking for them.

The Python is a constrictor. It uses its sharp, backward curving teeth to grasp and restrain prey. Then quickly coils its body around the prey and squeezes.

The Python doesn't actually seek to crush the prey and break bones. It constricts and suffocates its prey. But multiple fractures will occur when a beast is wrapped around prey and squeezed.

It squeezes so tightly that the animal can't breathe; each time the prey exhales, the python tightens its coils to take up space making the ribcage smaller and possibly crushing it.

After several tightening, the prey can't get air into its lungs, and at this point, the prey goes unconscious from lack of oxygen and blood to the brain.

This snake can also feel the heartbeat of the prey, and so continues to squeeze until the heart of the prey stops beating.

Death of the prey is primarily caused by cardiac arrest.

When the prey's heart stops, the snake knows it is safe to release its coils and begin to eat. It expands the jaws and swallows the prey whole.

So what's unique about the Python? What can we learn from it? Well, it's quite simple; you are supposed to be a Python. Yes, you who are reading this. You should and must be a Python.

Why should you be a Python? And how do you become one?

First, let's deal with the WHY.

It is because you are built for impact. You are not a waka pass in this movie called life.

There are three essential items you need to (positively) impact your society and the world, as well as achieve success. Two are internal; the third is external.

Your skill and your passion are the first two. The third is satisfying a human need, desire or want.

Next, the 'HOW.'

So how does becoming a python help you impact your society? Let's play with your mind a bit.

Imagine your gift/talent/skill as the prey, and your passion aka energy is the Python. Now wrap your energy/passion around your skill and squeeze. Each squeeze should produce an action.

As your skill exhales, squeeze a little more. Each breath equals another squeeze, and each squeeze leads to an action that should produce a new song, a new article, a new book, a new dance, a cloth, a fashion item, a service, a product etc.

Every day and all day, you should squeeze harder, tighter and only stop squeezing when the heart of your skill stops beating.

There is a market for every product, but there is no product for every market. This means that no matter what you squeeze out, it will satisfy a need, desire or want of someone, somewhere who requires what you produce. But how can they find you or know you if you don't produce anything?

Even if the world thinks what you do/produce is senseless or non-sense.

Please tell them there is always a sense in every nonsense and senselessness. Better still, tell them to say/use 'non-sense' and 'sense-less' without 'sense' and see if it makes a "sense tense," I mean, sentence.

So, till your heart stops beating, never stop squeezing. God bless.

CHAPTER SEVEN

LESSON FROM THE BABOONS!!!

Today let's talk about your cousins, you know the ones your Biology teacher told you that you evolved from. Do you remember?

Baboons are regarded as man's closest relative with the capability of reasoning and learning. They stand at

about 3ft tall and can weigh up to 100 pounds.

The Baboon is an aggressive, cunning and intelligent animal that will eat almost anything, including small mammals and birds.

They are social primates and live in groups of 30 to 50 with a dominant male leader and strict social hierarchy. Some groups could have up to 250 members, but the average size is fifty for most groups. Male dominance is determined by grunts and visual threats, followed by aggressive fights.

A group of baboons will put up a deadly fight to defend their own or to obtain food from other animals.

They sometimes attack people to take food, defend food or fight if they feel threatened. They are armed with 3-inch-long teeth (said to be the same size as a Lion) and powerful jaws. Their bite can easily penetrate the skin, break bones and even kill.

Baboons can climb trees, but don't live in trees. They prefer caves and are often found on the ground.

Aside from humans, the main predators they have are the big cats - Lions, Leopards and Cheetahs. Usually, if faced with just one big cat, male Baboons will display their teeth, yelling at the top of their voices. If that does not work, then they will fight if need be.

If faced with Lions, the Baboons run up a tree. But if faced with a Leopard, they flee from the tree (because Leopards can climb trees easily). One or two male Baboons can steal food from a Cheetah because the cat can't afford any form of injury.

A Baboon's yearly strategy is to feed, mate and stay alive.

That's all.

The Baboon's strategy is usually long term, e.g. 12 months. But they can have several tactics within one strategy. You should take a cue from this.

Baboons' tactic for staying alive is knowing which cat to run from, where to run to, when to fight and when it's dealing with a Cheetah, when to be a bully and steal food.

However, when the African wild dogs, aka Painted wolves, started hunting and killing Baboons, they were caught unawares. So instead of climbing trees, the Baboons fled on foot and the dogs easily caught and killed some.

At work, in business, in school, in relationships, in marriage, and life, some problems end up being seen as routine, and your response/reaction is on autopilot. But what do you do when a new, unseen problem/challenge arises and knocks you off your strides?

Start by reviewing your four "S": structure, strategy, skills and system.

Structure: Do you still have the right people in place? Do they have the necessary skills for this new challenge?

Strategy: Does the long-term plan address this new issue? Is there a need to change strategy, adopt new tactics or modify existing tactics?

Skills: Do you need new people with the required skills or just training? What training do our people need to implement the strategy or tactics to be used?

System: Also known as process flow - the question is how soon can we Implement the updated system? How do we ensure ease of process flow due to the changes introduced?

The African wild dogs hunt in packs and stand at just 2.5 ft. But their strength is in their numbers and ability to outlast a prey in a foot race. On the ground, they are faster than baboons.

Once the African wild dogs give chase, and the baboons run, they become easy pickings for the dogs. The moment a dog sinks his teeth into a baboon, fractions of seconds later, two or more pack members will grab different parts of the Baboon and literally rip it apart.

After a series of successful attacks by the dogs on them, the baboons began to adapt by changing their behaviour.

Instead of running from the dogs, the baboons would launch a counterattack by charging at the dogs and try to bite them. With time, the dogs began to sustain deep wounds from bites inflicted on them by the baboons.

Thus, it gradually became a dangerous pursuit for the dogs to hunt baboons.

New problems and challenges will always arise in life and business, and as long as you run from it, you will always be a victim.

The common saying is that, when the going gets tough, the tough get going!

Pray, tell me, going to where?

Please note that it is when the going gets tough, that the tough should seek collaboration.

Review your four "S", ask questions, seek answers, plan, upgrade your armour/ weapons/skills, work as a unit. Partner with people, collaborate, work your plan, execute your plan and then perfect the process.

Do what you need to do to win because winter is coming. Sorry, no winter in Africa, but you get the drift.

Don't let problems/challenges give you the runaround, learn from your cousins, the Baboons, stand and fight. After all, blood is thicker than water !!!

CHAPTER EIGHT

HOW DOES MARKETING RELATE TO A BEAST
THAT HAS A MOUTH FULL OF BACTERIA?

The Komodo Dragon, also known as the Komodo Monitor, is a specie of lizards found in the Indonesian Islands.

They are the most massive lizard species on Earth. They can grow as long as 10feet and weigh 70kg.   Given their location and size, they are at the top of the food chain, also known as apex predators of their ecosystem.

The Komodo Dragons are carnivores, feeding on large prey such as Deer, Water Buffaloes, Goats etc. They also feed on the decaying flesh of dead animals.

They have good vision and can run very fast over short distances. However, they are mainly ambush predators. Komodo Dragons wait for hours until a prey crosses their path, and then they rush at the prey, catching them unawares.

The Komodo has a unique way of killing its prey; all it takes is one bite.

Most times, after the prey is bitten, it is still able to run away. But the prey dies within 24 hours due to blood poisoning because the Komodo's saliva is said to contain about 50 strains of bacteria.

Once the prey is bitten, it experiences decreased blood pressure and increased blood loss. With time the prey goes into shock, rendering it too weak to fight, and death slowly but surely claims it.

With the Komodo's fantastic sense of smell, it is not always far behind the prey. It does not give chase; it just tracks the now-dead animal via smell and 'viola,' food is served.

One of my favourite marketing books is 'The Invisible Touch' by Harry Beckwith.

The book states, 'products are made; services are delivered. Products are used; services are experienced. Products have physical attributes we can evaluate before we buy; services do not even exist before we buy them, as we often pay for services in advance. Services are personal, and a service relationship touches our essence and reveals the people involved: provider and customer."

The Komodo's bite and tracking of its dead prey relates to two marketing concepts/principles from this book. They are:

1. What/where is your point of contact with your customer/audience.
2. To make and keep a sale, make and keep a powerful

connection.

The Komodo's point of contact with its prey is the bite. All it needs is one bite. All you need is to identify your point of contact with your customer/audience. For example, my people and I organise spoken word poetry events, so our point of contact is both emotional and physical.

The emotional point of contact is what the audience gets to hear/experience when they listen to poets performing on stage.

The physical part is me going to hug, shake and bump fists with the audience and poets, especially the poets, after the performance. I ensure to connect with them because for performers, all they need is a form of validation despite the applause of the audience.

We are humans, physical touch will always, always be necessary regardless of the ease of communication provided by technology.

I'm not saying go and be groping your customers o.

Your point of contact can be the packaging of your product/service, it can be the prompt response to enquiries and complaints or the confidence you exude in your area of competence.

As the Komodo tracks its now dead prey, it has built a somewhat relationship with it. Thus, the second concept of making and keeping a powerful connection, is all about relationship.

And like all healthy relationships, regular communication is key. Use your nose (aka the internet) to track them, e.g. Facebook birthdays, WhatsApp status message etc. People always like to talk/express themselves, so learn to be a 'monitoring spirit.'

There are tools online, e.g. Google alerts, which enable you to monitor key words spoken/typed online about you, your business, your market/Industry and your customers.

So like the Komodo Dragons, learn to bite, i.e. connect emotionally and/or physically. Also, it's important to learn to build a relationship with regular communication.

Have I helped you? Any questions? Clarification? Additional information? Or you need a hug?

I'm at your service.

CHAPTER NINE

IF A LION NEEDS 3CS, YOU NEED IT TOO!!!

Let's revisit the Lion and talk about the 3Cs and the 3Rs.

Are you ready? Okay, let's get it on. In a Pride of Lions, the male cub is more like a glorified tenant. There is no house, company or assets to inherit. The assets are the Lionesses and the location the

pride lives and hunts in. He is like matter that occupies space, and his position at the "BOD" meeting does not count. As an employee, he is there to follow the rules; his initiative is usually unappreciated. Sometimes that initiative gets him a query (slaps and bites) from the Lion King - his father, the MD.

The Lion King came into power, riding on blood and death. His reign can only end with his death. There is no stepping aside, and it is not a democracy. Also, weakness is not something that can or must be shown outwardly, except and perhaps with his queen(s).

The glorified tenant, the young Lion(s), only has a year or a two maximum to enjoy the luxury of belonging to a pride. Once he begins to show signs of sexual maturity, he is kicked out by his father.

The right to mate is earned via blood and death. It is never given; it is taken. The right to mate is just like power and clout that makes one a market/industry leader. You earn it; you don't inherit.

If the glorified tenant refuses to go, then he ends up dead. There can't be two kings ruling one kingdom. And based on assassination history, the son is no match for his father. If bets are placed, the odds are against the son, 100 to 0, because 10 out of 10 fights, he dies.

When the young Lion is kicked out of a pride, he is like a sacked employee or a startup business. If the young Lion is wise, he would have been participating in the hunt while he was in the pride. Such a lion would be like an employee with a side hustle because he would have hunting skills aka business experience.

Like every new business, the young lion faces two key challenges. These are:

1. Obscurity: People don't know you exist.

2. Seeming irrelevance: People know you exist, but you are an afterthought, you are not considered top 10 or even top 50.

How do you overcome obscurity and stay relevant? Overcoming these challenges will give the 3Rs. But first, you need the utilise the 3Cs to get the 3Rs.

What are the 3Rs and 3Cs? Don't worry; I will simplify it for you.

The 3Rs are:
1. Recognition (reputation, brand equity).
2. Reward (profit, inflow, business growth, revenue generation).
3. Recommendation (Referrals, word of mouth, increased customer base, viral content).

The young Lion goes into exile and will remain there until he can find and take over a pride. Thus, he needs to grow mentally (learn to stalk/ambush prey), which is the same as growing strategy and the right tactics, and physically to take down and kill prey (skill development). He needs to find strategic partners to align with his vision. Also, he needs to stay alive (i.e. keep business afloat) by avoiding lion Kings of other pride (i.e. debts, lack of liquidity, fraudsters, bad decisions).

If the young lion is lucky, he won't be the only male lion chased out by his father. Thus, if wise, he will quickly form a strategic alliance with his brothers. According to the good book, two are better than one. . .and a threefold cord is not quickly broken.

Taking over a pride equals blood and death. The resident Lion King won't go down without a fight. Thus, if you are going to overcome obscurity and stay relevant, the industry leaders won't be part of your cheerleaders. Business is War!!!

How do you overcome obscurity and stay relevant? You need the 3Cs, and these are:

1. Content (capacity, capability, skills, strategy, tactics etc.).
2. Collaboration (partners, cooperation, mentors, strategic alliances, structure etc.).
3. Community (market share, customers, distribution channel, system etc.)

The male Lion and his strategic partners usually spend about two years in exile before they can take over a pride. It might take longer for a single Lion.

Everyone faces the challenges of obscurity and the struggle for relevance at some point. This limits us from accessing the 3Rs. But with the proper implementation of the 3Cs, our chances of success are higher.

We can take this conversation further and one on one as regards the specific 3Cs you need for your industry. I'm always at your service.

Business is War, dominate dominate dominate!!!

CHAPTER TEN

A BIRD THAT CAN TAKE ON A LION.

W e will be talking about a bird next. This bird is able to face lions, leopards or hyenas and come out unhurt.

The truth is, a bird is a bird, so the ability to hold your own against would-be predators comes from deep within.

The fact is, you can't give what you don't have. So if it's not in you, you can't bring it.

These large, flightless birds have long, sturdy legs and a long, bare neck that protrudes from a round body covered with feathers. Males have a bold black-and-white colouring that they use to attract females, and the females are mostly brown.

Both sexes have small heads, a short, wide beak and big brown eyes protected by long dark lashes. They are found across Africa's hot savannahs and open woodland, the Ostrich, is the world's largest bird. It stands up to a massive 9 feet tall (especially the males) and weighs as much as 159 kg – the weight of two men combined!

The Ostrich is an interesting bird. It does not fly, because it is way bigger than an average bird. Like camels, the Ostrich can tolerate high temperatures and go without water for long periods.

The Ostrich might not be able to fly, but it can run! Using its long legs, powerful thighs and strong feet, this big bird can cover five metres in a single stride and reach speeds of over 70km per hour! Just one stride can be 10 to 16 feet (3 to 5 metres) long—that's longer than many rooms! When danger threatens, ostriches can escape easily by running away. Ostrich chicks can run at speeds approaching 35 miles per hour (56 kilometres per hour) at just a month old! When zooming along at such mega speed, the bird holds out its short wings to help it balance. Ostriches hold their wings out to help them balance when they run, especially if they suddenly change direction. Their primary use, though, along with the tail feathers, is for display and courtship. To show dominance, an ostrich holds its head up high and lifts its wings and tail feathers; to show submission, the head, wings, and tail hang down limply.

The amazing speed of the ostrich helps it outrun predators. This brilliant bird's strong legs don't only carry the ostrich where it wants to go – they are super effective when it comes to self-defence.

If an ostrich is cornered by a predator, e.g. Lion, Cheetah, Leopard or Hyena, the Ostrich can use its powerful legs to kick like a kangaroo. It will kick with a force powerful enough to kill or injure the predator. The Ostrich is the only bird that has two toes on each foot. The bird's two-toed foot is armed with a 4-inch claw on each foot, so predators can get hurt if the kick is well planted.

With their tall height and excellent eyesight, these fantastic creatures are great at spotting potential predators from afar. But if danger gets too close for comfort, the Ostrich will often lie low to hide, stretching its neck along the ground.

The colour of its feathers help it to blend in with the sandy soil where it lives. Have you ever heard that ostriches bury their head in the sand to hide? Well, as funny as that sounds, it is not true! But from far away, depending on what position the ostrich takes, it can sure look that way, hence how the myth began.
So, what is to be learnt from the ostrich. Power kicks?

Two things: courage comes from lack of choice, and you can't give what you don't have because what you need to excel is already in you or close to you.

When your business or career/profession, is down to a sink or swim decision, what do you do?

The action(s) we sometimes take that leads to greatness is often due to lack of options. You just have to survive, so you do whatever it takes.

An Ostrich would never set itself up with a Lion or other predators, but when such a situation arises, it is fight or die! If you were the Ostrich, would you rather die?

You can't give what you don't have. So feed your mind with more than enough information and knowledge, so you have more than enough to give.

Ostriches were born with strong legs, what are you born with? What can you do better than other people? What are your strong legs?

There is the market share, and there is a pocket share. Market share is the competition between people in the same industry.

The pocket share is the competition between people in different industries, due to the decision an individual makes between two totally different industries/products based on his pocket. For example, eat food or buy books, sleep and rest well or have sex, buy a car or travel abroad. How much of people's pocket (money) can you attract and get them to spend?

What you need to excel is already in you as potential or around you waiting to be discovered as an opportunity.

The good book says, 'Arise and shine for your light is come.' This means to work on yourself using knowledge and information. Perfect your craft and continually 'loud it' for the world to see and hear.

I was called the loudest poetry promoter in Nigeria by EGC. Whether praise or yab, I don't care, because I'm about to crank up the volume. I go deaf una ear, just wait for my ostrich legs to start kicking. I'm going to kick the doors and windows down.

I have just two options, make it or make it. And what I will use is what I have in me.

What are your options? What do you have? Be an ostrich; your legs are your PowerPoint, Excel with it.

Flight or fight, the choice is yours. But never forget, you can always give what you have. It's in you, learn and figure out how to give it, excellently and perfectly.

In case you are unsure of what your ostrich legs are, I'm at your service. I hope this made sense. If not, why did you read it?

CHAPTER ELEVEN

WINNING IN BUSINESS LIKE A
RESIDENT COBRA HITMAN

The Mongoose is a small rodent-like mammal naturally found in Asia, Africa and parts of Europe. It is a short-legged animal with a pointed nose, small ears and a long furry tail. Its fur

is grey to brown and is commonly grizzled or flecked with lighter grey.

An adult size Mongoose ranges between 7 inches to 28 inches (without measuring the tail) and depending on the species.

Mongooses live in burrows that they rarely dig them themselves; instead, they opt to move into vacant burrows left by other animals.

Mongooses eat plants, small mammals, birds, reptiles and eggs. They also attack and kill poisonous snakes, as they appear to be almost immune to the poison of a snake.

Mongooses are extremely quick and agile, which allows them to effectively dodge the snake attacks with relative ease. They usually adopt a matrix style dodge/manoeuvre when facing the King Cobra or the Black Mamba.

Mongooses dodge the snake's attacks continuously while waiting for the snake to tire. Then they dart at the head of the snake and crack the skull with a powerful bite.

The King Cobra (between 10 to 18 feet) and the Black Mamba (maximum length of 14 feet) are easily the biggest snakes in the class of the most deadly and poisonous snakes in the world. These two snakes are fast too.

Yet, the Mongoose has successfully killed both on separate occasions time and again.

One of the books I love to always re-read for ideas on Business, Marketing and dealing with Competition is REWORK by Jason Fried and David H Hansson.

Three key points on dealing with competition from the book are:

1. Pick a fight
2. Don't outspend, out-teach.
3. Decommoditise your product.

Let's start with the first point: pick a fight. The King Cobra and Black Mamba are not prey, they are predators. Even big cats like lions won't mess with these snakes, because they will get bitten.

The Mongoose is small, agile and quick. Also, snake venom doesn't easily penetrate the fur of the mongoose.

If you think a competitor sucks, say so. When you do that, you'll find others who agree with you and will rally to your side. Taking a stand always stands out because people get excited by conflict. They take sides, passion is ignited, and society takes notice of you. It also gives you a great story to tell your customers.

Please note, sometimes, once in a while (or "two whiles"), the mongoose does not win against these big poisonous snakes.

So pick your fights carefully.

Two, don't try to outspend, outsell or out-sponsor competitors, try to out-teach them. Depending on your line of business, you can replace out-teach with out-work or out-manoeuvre your competitors.

The Mongoose does not stay still, waiting for snakes; it is constantly on the move. It's small and faster. Quick decisions and quick actions are required to out-wit your bigger competitors.

Out-teaching is a whole new level of connection with your customers. It allows you to earn loyalty, trust, respect and new fans. No matter what you do, you know something other people don't. If you are in business, you have more experience than people waiting to start their own. So there is always, always something to teach.

Personally, I do a lot of studying and research on the business of

Spoken Word Poetry, and love to share information and knowledge of what I'm about to decipher, which is why I write often.

Now to number three, decommoditise your product. If you are successful, people will try to copy what you do. So you should become the competitive advantage, by making yourself a part of your product or service.

Pour yourself into your product/service and everything around your business: how you sell it, how you support it, how you explain it, and how you deliver it. Competitors can never copy the you in your product.

The Mongoose is not the only meat-eating mammal in the wild, but most bigger and faster animals, can't successfully kill snakes. There is a distinct personal signature to how the Mongoose delivers service.

As regards distinct personal signature, I consider myself a nurturer, so I'm always seeking ways to promote and help poets, especially the younger ones.

In closing, become a 'resident Cobra hitman' like the Mongoose. Be a force to reckon with.
However, don't get overconfident, for snakes can still land deadly bites when they feel too threatened. And you know your competition did not come to the business to play.

Any questions?
Well, answers are not guaranteed.

But ask all the same so I can give you homework!!!

CHAPTER TWELVE

DO WOLVES DO SIDE-CHICKS???

Wolves are the largest members of the dog family. They live and hunt in packs and roam vast distances to hunt. They are highly territorial animals, and territory size depends on the availability of prey.

A wolf pack's average size ranges from 3 to 30. The pack is headed by a dominant couple, a male and female known as the alpha couple. The dominant couple are the only ones allowed to mate and breed. This means simply that other members of the pack live like nuns and monks, or leave the pack to form theirs. This usually is the case for male wolves.

The Wolf is the apex predator in Alaska (USA), Canada and Asia. Bears are the only other animal who challenge the supremacy of wolves. One on one, a bear will kill a wolf. So it will take a pack of wolves to take down a Bear.

The Wolf is built for travel. Its long legs, large feet, and deep but narrow chest suit it well for life on the move. It has keen senses, large canine teeth, powerful jaws and the ability to pursue prey over long distances when on the hunt.

A male wolf is averagely 6 ft long, stands at 30 inches tall at the shoulder and can weigh up to (and above) 65kg. The female wolf is usually smaller than the male.

Wolves can kill their prey effectively because of their strong jaws, which can break bones in just a few bites. They eat only meat and feed on anything from the smallest animal, e.g. mice, to the biggest animal, e.g. the Musk Oxen and the largest species within the deer family, namely, the Moose and Elk.

It's during a hunt that the co-operation, collaboration and team-work between a pack of wolves is clearly demonstrated. Wolves can trail their prey for days before making a move.

During the hunt before the chase, the Wolves assess the herd, looking for signs of weakness. They also factor in the weather and the terrain, as wolves are more of endurance runners and not speed merchants.

They don't kill their prey; they capture the prey and start eating. The prey usually dies from shock, muscle damage or blood loss.

They will follow/chase their prey all day and all night if need be. They have a highly organised social structure which enables them enjoy maximum cooperation when hunting, communicating and defending territory.

The Alpha Wolves eat first. Failure to adhere to this might mean death to the disobedient Wolf.

In forming a pack, once a lone roaming wolf has found a mate, they usually stay together for life, i.e. till death do them part.

Communication is essential for animals that live together in family groups, like wolves. Communication helps maintain social stability.

For wolves, there are non-vocal forms of communication to show dominance or submission. While vocal communication includes growls, howls, barks, whines, yips, whimpers, and snarls.

So what can we learn from the wolves?

1. Have a commitment strategy, and not an exit strategy: Have this strategy in marriage, in business, in relationship and life generally. Like the alpha couple of a wolf pack, and like wolves on the hunt, stay committed to the very end. However, recognise and acknowledge when you need to quit, e.g when there is a threat to life.

2. Collaboration, cooperation and teamwork are essential for success: A lone wolf usually won't take on a bigger animal as prey, so it deals only with preys aka project(s) that are smaller and that it can handle alone. But small projects handled by one man don't usually generate big returns or make big impact. Life is best lived with others.

What the wolves lack in size, power and weapons, they make up for with collaboration and intelligence. As animals, they know and value the importance of cooperation and teamwork; so should you.

3. Communicate always and give respect to earn respect: I love my woman very much, but occasionally, I remind her I'm not a mind reader. Because assumptions will simply make an "ass of you and me." So, the lesson here is to communicate communicate communicate!!! Vocal communication please. We can't all read moods and body language.

The alpha couple are usually the ones with the strongest leadership skills and organise the pack to hunt as a group. Thus, wolves understand their place in the line of authority and understand that (true) respect is earned and not demanded. For wolves who step out of line, they get attacked by the alpha male or other members of the pack and/or get chased out.

Learn to give respect to get respect. However, you can't give what you don't have. But like most things, it starts from within, so learn to have respect for self, and you can extend it outward.

Has this been worth your while? What else did you get from this aside from the three things I pointed out?

CHAPTER THIRTEEN

THE ZEBRA, THE STOOL
AND THE THREE LEGS.

F odder is food fed to domestic animals.

But when you live in the jungle and you are called a lion fodder? What would be your vision statement?

Zebras are several species of African equids (horse family) identified by their distinct black and white striped coats. Zebra stripes come in different patterns, unique to each one. They are generally social animals that live in small harems to large herds. In small harems, a group of female zebras share a single male zebra.

Unlike their closest relatives, horses and donkeys, zebras have never been truly domesticated. They are sturdy, spirited animals: willful and playful, social and standoffish, resilient and vulnerable. Their life in a herd can be complex, but they also find safety in numbers.

They have excellent hearing and eyesight. Although they are slower than horses, their great stamina helps them outpace predators. When chased, a zebra will zig-zag from side to side, making it difficult for the predator.

They are prey to almost all the African predators, e.g. lion, African wild dogs, hyena, crocodile etc. However, they are not cowards when it comes to defending themselves.

They are usually 4.2 to 5 feet tall and weigh 550 to 990 pounds. Like horses, they walk, trot, canter and gallop. But they have a different temperament to horses. They are far more aggressive and a lot more dangerous. They have been known to kick each other to death.

To survive in the African jungle where they are on the menu list of most predators, Zebras have a vision statement: to survive by any means necessary, flight or fight.

Based on their vision statement, Zebras have evolved into alert, responsive animals that flee in the face of danger but also possesses a powerful response when cornered/captured.

The first book I have read and finished for the year 2019 is *Risk and Return* by Yomi Jemibewon. It was a mind igniting, eye-opening, and brain fingering read. I think the zebras have read it too or are co-authors.

The book states: Define a personal vision for your business/career and be honest with yourself about the areas you need to work on. Think of this vision as a stool you need to build and determine what three legs are required for your stool to become sturdy and firm. Make sure every job or role you take either helps strengthen an existing leg or helps build 'a leg' that you don't already have.

Let me ask, do you have a stool? What makes up the three legs of your stool?

The zebras' tool is to survive by all and any means necessary. So, what constitutes the three legs of the Zebra's stool?

1. Stamina/strength/speed: to outrun predators.
2. Kicks: the zebras have a powerful kick that can break a Lion's

jaw. So when chased or cornered, they kick out.

3. Bite: Zebras are savage biters. When captured, they will chomp on the capturer. Let me remind you that teeth to the skin is not like a comb to hair. And the skin of most mammals is very sensitive.

Now, I who am writing, what is my own stool and three legs?

Vision: Own the biggest poetry slam franchise in the world (and bestselling author in more 75 countries of the world).

The three legs are:

1. Competence: mental capacity, e.g. knowledge information, and physical capability, e.g. organising events.
2. Content: Well, you are reading Chapter 11 or 12 of my 4th e-book.
3. Capital/Investment/Funding.

I have the first and second legs covered; I'm working on the 3rd leg.

Want to share your stool and three legs with me? Or perhaps, you need figuring it out?

I'm always at your service. Jah bless and Shalom!!!

CHAPTER FOURTEEN

After compiling over ten chapters of business lessons derived from the animal world, I thought I should give it a rest.

However, I was surfing the internet when I saw a picture, which led to me seeing several videos and

it became clear that I had to write again.

The Jaguar is the third-largest cat in the world,
exceeded in size by the tiger and lion. It can weigh up

to 100kg and has a body length of 5ft 6 inch.

The Jaguar has a compact body, a broad head and powerful jaws.
Though it looks like the Leopard, it is taller and far more power-
fully built than the Leopard. The spots on both cats are also distinct and different when viewed closely.

Jaguars have incredibly powerful jaws, strong enough to pierce
skulls and crack a sea turtle's shell. They are fearsome predators
and will hunt anything from frogs, fish, crocodiles, alligators to
livestock, cows and deer.

Jaguars have the strongest bite force of any big cat (relative to its
size). While they employ deep throat bite and suffocation technique typical among big cats, it sometimes uses a killing method
unique amongst cats. It pierces the bones directly at the sides and
base of the skull between the ears of prey with its canine teeth,
piercing the brain.

The skull bite enables the Jaguar to successfully kill reptiles such
as crocodiles and alligators, by leaping on the back of the prey
and severing the bone beneath the skull, which immobilises the
target.

Unlike most big cats, the Jaguar loves the water; it swims, bathes,
plays and hunts in streams and pools. It can also climb trees, but
unlike the Leopard, the Jaguar can't carry its prey while climbing

a tree.

A Jaguar is the apex predator in the jungle where it is located. It has no direct competition (except other Jaguars). Jaguars are mostly (and only) found in the jungle of Central and Southern America. They often ride solo as jaguars only come together in mating season, and in a mother and child relationship.

What are the business lessons here? We can pick three or four from the jaguar. These are:

1. Location: The Leopard (which is similar but smaller to the Jaguar) is located in both African and Asian jungles. In Africa, the Leopard has to face other predators like Lions, Hyenas, Wild Dogs etc, while in the Asian jungle, the Leopard has to compete with the Tiger and Bear for prey.

The Jaguar rules the jungle; it is a market leader. With no direct competitors, it determines the economy of the jungle and dominates other predators, including the Anaconda. Location is key to business; it has a direct effect on its future success or failure. So pick your location wisely.

2. USP (Unique Selling Point): Lions and Tigers (the biggest cats) rarely get to kill big reptiles such as Crocodiles and Alligators, because their throat biting and suffocation/killing technique won't work for big reptiles. How do you get to the throat of a Crocodile without it biting you?

However, the Jaguar's USP is the skull biting technique. Pierce the skull, puncture the brain or sever the bone connecting the brain and spine and it is lights out for the crocodile. What is your USP? What makes you easily do what others struggle to do?

Find it, learn it, perfect it and you will eat crocodiles. By that, I mean you will profit a lot.

3. Risk taking: Going into the water to hunt and kill crocodiles is a risk; the table can turn against the jaguar, and it usually does. However, to get that special deal, you need to take risks. Leave that comfort zone, go where others won't dare, do what others think impossible and become a force to reckon with. No pain, no gain; know pain, know gain.

The fourth would be niche marketing, but these three should suffice for you.

Even if you forget all I wrote, don't forget this: Find your unique selling point; cultivate it, perfect it and deploy it.

CHAPTER FIFTEEN

THE TIGER AND THE NEED FOR AN
EFFECTIVE BUSINESS SYSTEM

M r Tiger is an apex predator. It is prey to none
but eats all other animals
as food. Currently, Tigers are found
in Southeast Asia, China and Rus-
sia. The Tiger is the largest cat species, easily recognised for its pattern
of vertical stripes on reddish-orange

fur with a lighter underside.

The Tiger has a muscular body with powerful forelimbs, a large head and a tail that is about half the length of the body. The tail helps the tiger in executing sharp turns. The length of a tiger ranges between 8 feet to 13 feet, and it can weigh between 90kg to 300kg. From the ground up to the shoulder, it stands between 2.3 feet to 4 feet. Although it is shorter than the Lion, the tiger is greater in length and weight. The muscles of the tiger has no rival among other big cats.

Tigers are fiercely territorial and generally solitary, except during mating season and when females bear young cubs. The cubs usually leave their mum after two years. The Tiger is one of the few big cats that likes the water and is a powerful swimmer. Their night vision is six times better than humans, so they usually hunt alone at night. However, Tigers are are also opportunists and won't pass up the chance of a daytime meal if and when available. Tigers are ambush hunters who prefer to sneak up on their prey before exploding into action, killing them with a bite to the neck or back of the head. They have large, padded feet that make it easy to stalk prey silently.

It is stated that the hind legs of a tiger are longer than the front legs, making it possible to leap forward 20 to 30 feet in one jump. They are not the fastest runners amongst the big cats and also can only run for short distances. Tigers mainly hunt Deer, Wild Boar, Buffalo, Antelope, Elephant, Calf etc. However, a lone tiger can take down a prey four or five times its size, no matter how large and dangerous the prey is, e.g. Gaur (largest wild cattle species in the world), Elephant etc. Lions are the second biggest cats in the world, and a lone lion is usually unable to take down a buffalo, not to now mention an elephant.

So, how is the Tiger able to successfully tackle prey much bigger than its size?

The Tiger, like a well-planned business, utilises the 4 's', namely: structure, strategy, skills and system. The structure of a tiger is like that of a sole proprietor. Unlike the Lion who is more aligned to partnership business and/or Limited Liability Companies. The strategy of a tiger for business continuity is: hunt, kill prey, eat, have sex, and defend territory, all year, every year. The skill set of the Tiger is defined by its body structure. They are:

1. Muscular body with powerful forelimbs to grab, hold and swipe. The swipe of a tiger is powerful enough to smash a Buffalo's skull.
2. Longer hind legs for leaping towards a prey.
3. Large padded feet for silent stalking.
4. Large head with a powerful bite force (second to the Jaguar).

Quickie before the 4th and last 'S':
What is your business structure?
What is your strategy for the year?
What is your skill set?

The 4th 'S' is a system, and this is our core focus. Online sources state that a system includes procedures, processes, methods or course of action designed to achieve a specific result.

Systems serve as the essential building blocks and support that allows different functions and departments to interact with each other and connect them to the operational strategy of the business.

The business system of a tiger can be broadly categorised into five stages. These are:
1. Detection: locate and stalk prey.
2. Attack: ambush prey.
3. Capture: subdue and kill prey.
4. Consumption: eat and store to eat later.
5. Defend territory

The business system of the Tiger ties into its overall strategy. So over and over again, the Tiger utilises its well-oiled system to get food for itself. In business, well-oiled systems are used to generate profit.

It is said that only one out of ten hunts/attack by the Tiger is successful. This is true in line with the law of averages (of marketing/prospecting for customers). So, if for every ten, you get one. This means If you do 100, you'll get 10. So increase the number of trials to increase your rate of success.

Important question: Which system is in place to help you achieve your strategy?
Do you have or even know how to build a system?

Pray tell. What are the elements of your business system?

An effective business system is expected to have the following elements:
1. Planning
2. Budgeting/resources management
3. Marketing
4. Building a team
5. Customer service
6. Sales
7. Continuous improvement.

If a tiger needs an effective system to profit, what about you?

Do you need help to set up an effective system?

CHAPTER SIXTEEN

THE PUFF ADDER AND IT'S BUSINESS POSITIONING STRATEGY

T he Puff Adder is one of Africa's deadliest snake species, not only due to its deadly venom but also because of the stealth, it displays in ambushing prey.

The Puff Adder belongs to the family of Vipers and can grow between 3ft to 6ft in length. It has a stumpy, robust build and a large triangular head. Its head is much wider than the neck. The average weight of an adult Adder can be up to five kilograms. Males are larger than females. The colouration of the snake differs from region to region.

It is often termed a sluggish snake and relies on camouflage for protection. Its movement is in the mode of that of a caterpillar, which is aided by its weight (muscles) for traction. When agitated, it can move with surprising speed in the usual serpentine movement of snakes. The Puff Adder is a good swimmer and can also climb with ease. Like most vipers, Puff Adders have hinged fangs through which venom is injected into prey. During a strike, the force of the impact is so strong, and the long fangs penetrate so deeply that the prey is often killed by the physical trauma alone. The fangs apparently can penetrate soft leather. They can strike to a distance of about one-third of their body length. But some will launch their entire body forward in the process. The snake does not usually grip its prey; it releases quickly to return to the striking position.

Puff Adders are known for their aggressive temperament, and when threatened, they take a tightly coiled defensive posture with the forepart of their body held in a taut S shape. Then they inflate their upper body and hiss. This habit led to the snake being called Puff Adder. When a Puff Adder hisses, and you don't adhere to the hissing, it strikes. Without quick treatment, death is sure.

Recent studies and video footage show that the Puff Adder is not only an ambush predator but knows how to attract prey to itself. It uses different types of techniques to attract its prey. That's exactly how businesses should know how to get customers by using different methods to bring customers your way.

For customers such as frogs, the snake will camouflage itself and start to use and move its tongue like an insect/worm. It mimics an insect/worm movement by wagging its tongue slowly and deliberately to attract nearby amphibians, i.e. frogs, toads etc. Frogs like to eat insects and worms. So like a hungry customer, the Frog goes for the meal. Once the Frog is within striking distance, the Puff Adder strikes, and the Frog ends up with a venom-filled body. The snake swallows it after it dies.

For another class of customers such as birds, the Puff Adder will camouflage and start to wave its tail in the air like a worm. Any hungry bird that comes close ends up on the meal list.

For another class of customers, such as small rodents, attraction to position won't work, so proper positioning is key. The snake will have to wait for the rat to come close to it. Thus, the Puff Adder has to know where to stay, so that the rat will stray to it.

Two Quick principles we can glean from the Puff Adder are as follows:
1. What is your positioning strategy?
2. How well do you know your 'starving crowd?'

An effective positioning strategy considers the strengths and weaknesses of the organisation, the needs of the customers and the position of Competitors.
Positioning is a market concept that outlines what a business should do to market its product and services to customers. In positioning, an image is created for the product based on the intended audience/customer.

We've touched on positioning, let's focus a bit on the starving crowd. I first came across this in the book titled, Small Business, Big Money by Akin Alabi.

The concept of the starving crowd is originally from the Gary Halbert letters.
If you sell food, what you need the most is a starving crowd. They don't care if the food is sweet or not; they just want to eat. But first, you need to locate/ identify and know/ understand them. Fact is, there is a market for every product, but no product for every market.

So find your starving crowd, know your starving crowd, so that you will be well-positioned to know what to serve them.

The power of understanding your starving crowd is amazing. It's like shooting a rifle with telescopic sight instead of a shotgun.

Who is your audience? Can you meet their needs and satisfy their wants?

First, know your starving crowd.

Next, position yourself to serve them well.

The Puff Adder can tell the difference between frogs and birds, it knows each prey's food, where and how the prey seeks for food, and it knows how to attract them differently. To eat rats, it's all about the puff adder getting the positioning right.

In the Bible, Esau is an example of a 'starving crowd.'
But are you 'Jacob-ed' to take advantage of this?

Selah.

N.B. 'Jacob-ed' is a synonym of 'positioned.'

CHAPTER SEVENTEEN

WHO LIKES BED BUGS? NO ONE?

 k, who likes
cockroaches? Anyone?

Well, I don't like them either, but I've come to respect them. Why? They teach digital footprints and more.

Digital footprints are basically the traceable digital activities (that you) manifest on the internet or on digital devices. It can be passive and/or active.

People leave digital footprints online knowingly and unknowingly, for good or bad, it makes you unique, searchable and researchable online.

How do you knowingly leave digital footprints? Well, how do bed bugs spread? They get spread, i.e. carried around from place to place by people via clothes, bags and other items. So get people to share you/your content online. The more the share, the more you spread like bed bugs into corners no one would have expected you to be. You know you got a bed bug problem when you get the itch time and time again, and it's not mosquitoes. I prefer mosquito to bed bugs.

Digital footprints can be for your good or bad, i.e. come to harm you via the release of sensitive information not meant for public consumption.

So how do you erase unwanted digital footprints? Well, do you know cockroaches eat bed bugs? Cockroaches search out and delete/deactivate bed bugs.

Maybe cockroaches are your friends after all.

CHAPTER EIGHTEEN

YOU WILL NOT OUT KISS ME!!!

One of my favourite speakers, E.T. the hip hop preacher is fond of saying (more like shouting) 'you will not out work me.' This itself is a strategy if you adopt or flip the word 'work' into something else.

There is one animal that has only one strategy when it comes to hunting. But time and time again, it always works. Perhaps, I should say one out of ten times, which is termed the law of averages (more on this law much later).

This animal is smaller than the Lion, Hyena, Leopard, German Shepherd...you get the drift. So its success is not a function of size.

This animal is not as fast as a Cheetah; even an Antelope is faster than this animal. Yet time and time again, it feeds on Antelopes.

This animal is what you would call a local dog, but in documentaries, it's called the African dog. They hunt in packs, but this is not their key strength.

So when my favourite speaker says, you will not outwork me. I see the African dogs say; you will not outrun me.
The strategy of the African dogs is simple, year in year out. Identify the target, and give chase that's all. No fuss, no complications, no big grammar. Simplicity is the best complexity.

What is your own strategy for the current term? Can you explain it to yourself and then your partners without complexity?

Why does this Strategy work? Because the African Dogs know their SWOT. They are not big enough to wrestle bigger prey, e.g. buffalo. But they can run long distance without getting tired. This is their strength, and they use it over and over again.

They identify their target and give chase. You will not outrun me they scream to the antelope. The antelope runs, and each time it looks back, the dogs are there, not even breaking a sweat.

You will not outrun me, the dogs scream. The Antelope is tired; the legs are faltering, it can't go on. But to stop is certain death.

The Antelope stops, the legs can no longer go on. The dogs catch up. They start to eat the animal alive. The dogs can't waste time. If a lion or a hyena comes along, it will take away their food. So they eat on the run.

Five minutes later, only hoofs and horns are left. It was another successful hunt for the dogs simply because you will not outrun them.

I might not perform as well as you do, I might not dance, sing, rap, draw, talk, paint, box, kick or kiss ass well as you do. But this year, my battle cry is simple; you will not outwrite me.

That's my simple plan, what is yours?

CHAPTER NINETEEN

THE GAME OF THRONES
AND SWOT ANALYSIS

When it comes to SWOT analysis, there is a scene in the Game of Thrones show that played over and over

in my mind and best illustrate the adoption of SWOT into an actionable strategy and tactics.

Let me give a brief background of the scene:

A young lady (let's call her Puma) was training to be an assassin. The main trainer was a man, and there was an older female student (let's call her Bilikisu) who did not like Puma and often bullied her.

Due to over eagerness, Puma went blind at a time and had to sleep on the street, in a dark room under the bridge. While Puma was blind, Bilikisu daily engaged her in a sword fight, beat and bullied her thoroughly. For one, Bilikisu was a superior fighter; two, Puma was blind.

After a while, Puma regained her sight, but when sent on an assassination assignment, she did not carry it out. So a hit was placed on her head, and guess who the hitman, sorry, hit woman was You guessed right, Bilikisu.

Day after day, Puma ran from Bilikisu to avoid getting killed, because Puma knew she could not beat Bilikisu in a fair sword fight.

However, one day, while Puma was being pursued by Bilikisu, she (Puma) ran into the darkroom under the bridge. There was a single candle on. Bilikisu entered the room, locked the door and draw out her sword. Puma picked up her sword and waited for Bilikisu to draw close to her, and just as the sword fight was about to begin, Puma flicked her sword at the candle and effectively put off the light. Now the whole room was dark, no single light and the door was locked, no outside help.

Guess who won.

Yes, you're right again, Puma.

And that, my people, is SWOT analysis and adopting SWOT into actionable strategy/tactic.

IN CLOSING...

Funny how the mind works.
I spend hours watching Nat Geo Wild.
I spent a fortune buying books on business, strategy, marketing, and the likes. I equally invest time reading the books.
The mind now found a way to merge two obviously different and unrelated things.
Who created the mind?
My father who art in heaven, the real MVP.
He is the boss.
Me? I'm his bus.

REFERENCES:

Nat Geo WILD

Nationalgeographic.com

Google.com

Wikipedia

YouTube

LiveScience.com

Britannica.com

Krugerpark.co.za

Animals.sandiegozoo.org

Quora

Awf.org/wildlife-conservation

whateats.com

compareanimal.com

thoughtco.com/hippo-facts-4142336

http://www.ox.ac.uk/news/2015-12-21-cecil-lion-donors-give-more-%C2%A3750k-11m-wildlife-research

www.asiaone.com/asia/singaporean-tourist-bitten-komodo-dragon

www.adventuresportsnetwork.com/random/lion-cubs-greeted-with-roars-in-first-meeting-with-dad/

www.whitewolfpack.com/2014/12/10-pictures-of-growling-wolves-that.html

http://rennersafaris.com/2015-04-african-safari-photos-from-tanzania-and-kenya-newsletter/

https://www.wits.ac.za/news/latest-news/research-news/2017/2017-02/a-lure-at-both-ends---puff-adders-leave-nothing-to-chance.html

https://www.tanzania-experience.com/

https://www.sabisabi.com/wildfacts/

https://www.pexels.com/

https://www.nytimes.com/2016/04/24/arts/television/hbo-game-of-thrones-arya-interview.html

OTHER BOOKS BY OLUMIDE HOLLOWAY

1. The Way of the Lion.

2. Smoking Guns and Bleeding Streets.

3. The Untold Story of Uriah the Hittite.

4. Storytelling the Book of Proverbs.

5. The Poetpreneur.

6. Love Letters from a Poetpreneur.

7. Darkness can be very dark.

8. How many NO, make a YES?

All the books are available on Amazon.

The books are also on www.wordup411ng.com, and do subscribe to the website to receive notifications of news and updates by email.

THE WAY OF THE LION.

CHAPTER ONE

"Mister Tenant, your days are numbered. Hope you have packed your load" Tete said mockingly as she passed by his side and patted his rump with her paw.

"Get off me," he snarled.

He leaped up to lunge at her. But out of the corner of his eyes, he caught sight of her mother and his other three stepmothers watching them keenly.

His anger rapidly subsided and he walked away from his half-sister.

"Hey Didi, where are you running to? You scared of your own tail?" Tete called out.

"Enough! Tete," her mother snapped.

"I was just joking with him."

"Enough! I said."

"But Didi is still going to leave, right?"

"Yes, our custom demands we send him away from the Pride. But, don't make an enemy of him, for your paths might still cross."

"He won't last a day on his own," Tete replied.

"Never say never," said her mother quietly.

"He is a wimp."

"Your father was once like him."

"My father is a warrior," Tete said.

"Yes, he is. But he was not born one. He became one."

"Didi does not have the balls."

"He will grow it."

"How?"

"Lack of options often makes a hero of the weakest of us."

"He can't even hunt on his own."

"He will learn."

"Who will teach him when he leaves the Pride?"

"Time and chance happen to us all. Life will teach him using hunger and loneliness."

"I still don't agree with you mum. You don't know Didi."

"I have been a Lion longer than you have been my child. I know Lions and I know a warrior when I see one."

"Hmm."

"My child, your father is my 3rd husband. I have seen many things that your mind is yet to understand. So be careful not to make an enemy of your brother."

"Even if he comes back, I will be ready for him."

"No my child, if he comes back, he will be too much for you."

THE WAY OF THE LION.

CHAPTER TWO

Didi walked away from the Lionesses. He knew when the time comes; they will join his father to attack him. The thought of being an outcast made him shiver.

"How will I survive?" Didi asked aloud, "what if I decide to stay?"

He had two options, leave gently or fight his father for the right to stay. His mind flashed back to a year earlier.

He had had two older half-brothers, Kini and Niki. He was quite close to them and loved to always hang out with them.

However, Kini had tried to mate with one of the Lionesses, and their father, Daka, had seen him.

Thus, their father had demanded that Kini and Niki left the pride. But Kini stood his ground and Niki backed him up. He had watched as their father took the two of them on and in minutes, the fight was over.

Kini lost an eye and Niki ended up with a broken spine. Niki died within 2 days and Kini died 2 days later from hunger or an infection or maybe both.

"I can't fight Father," Didi said to himself, "I will be dead in seconds."

He watched as his 3 younger half-brothers played with their mother. He was older than them. And at just a year old, it would be another 12 months before they also became outcasts. His own eviction was just a matter of days or maybe hours.

Twice, his father had chased him when he tried to feed on the animals hunted and killed by the Lionesses. So he had had to wait for his father, the Lionesses, and other cubs to finish eating before he could eat.

"They are lucky to have each other," Didi whispered as he remembered his siblings and mother.

About 18 months earlier, his siblings, a brother, and two sisters, as well as his mother, had been killed in a hunt gone wrong. The Pride had ambushed a herd of Buffalo that was grazing close to the den. The cries of the Buffalo they caught in the stampede had attracted the other Buffaloes to come back. The herd, led by the bulls, had attacked the Lions and chased them right into the den. His siblings were trampled to death while his mother bled to death from being gored. Didi grew up being cared for by the other Lionesses.

"Maybe I should leave before they chase me away," Didi deliberated, "at least it will be on my terms."

Suddenly, he felt chills that made the hair stand up on his neck. Didi looked up and saw his father, Daka, staring at him about 100 meters away.

He stood up looking at his father for what seemed like an hour but actually was just a minute. As he watched, his father started to move slowly towards him.

Didi looked at his right and saw the Lionesses were now paying close attention to the scene.

"Has my time come?" Didi thought in terror, "fight or flight?"

Slowly, the distance between him and his father disappeared.

(The Way of the Lion is an epic tale of love, lust and loss).

COPYRIGHT

THE END.

www.ingramcontent.com/pod-product-compliance
Lightning Source LLC
Chambersburg PA
CBHW020600220526
45463CB00006B/2382